THE RIDICULOUSLY SIMPLE GUIDE TO TRELLO

A BEGINNERS GUIDE TO PROJECT MANAGEMENT WITH TRELLO

SCOTT LA COUNTE

RIDICULOUSLY
SIMPLE BOOKS

ANAHEIM, CALIFORNIA

www.RidiculouslySimpleBooks.com

Table of Contents

Disclaimer: *Please note, while every effort has been made to ensure accuracy, this book is not endorsed by Atlassian Corporation Plc. and should be considered unofficial.*

INTRODUCTION

Working as a team can be challenging, but working remotely as a team can add a layer of complexity to the work; it can be difficult to monitor who is working on (or responsible for) different aspects of a project and where they are in terms of deliverables. Trello, which is a part of the enterprise software development company Atlassian, is a Kanban-style project management tool that can run natively on your computer or on the web.

Trello lets you work collaboratively wherever you are and whatever you are working on. There are free and paid versions of the software, so it works for any budget and any company regardless of size. It also integrates with the software you already have.

[1]

WELCOME TO TRELLO

This chapter will cover:
- What makes Trello unique
- How to sign up
- Changing background

THE BASICS

To get started, head to https://trello.com and sign up for a free account.

The sign-up is a breeze. You can sign up with your email or just use your Google, Microsoft, or

Apple account to login. Personally, I prefer to use one of those three to login because it will be one less password to remember.

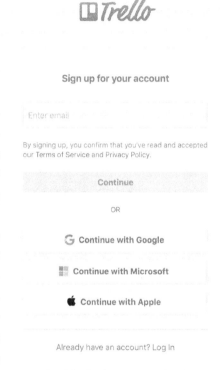

You'll get a confirmation about who you are (you'll also get an email—emails will come from Taco, which is probably one of the stranger email senders you'll have in your inbox). Depending on how you are signing in, you'll probably have an extra layer of verification you'll need to add (i.e. a verification code).

Create your account

@gmail.com

Full name

By creating an account, I accept the Atlassian Cloud Terms of Service and acknowledge the Privacy Policy.

Create your account

Already have an Atlassian account? Log in

That's it! You'll now get a very brief onboarding tutorial. Here you can create your first board (Don't worry! You can delete it).

You'll probably have several boards. You may have one for your sales team, one for your admin team, etc. Within those boards, you'll have different lists. Within that list, you'll have different cards.

Add the name of your board. I'm just going to call it my vacation planning board.

Click the grey button; it will turn blue when you do this. When ready, hit the blue button to go to the next step.

Next, you can start naming your lists. You'll be able to start with three, but you can add more later. You'll notice as you do this, there will be a preview that changes.

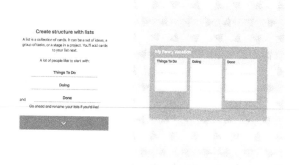

Next, you can start naming those cards within your to-do list.

As you do so, you'll again get a preview of the changes on the right side.

Finally, you can add details within the list—this will be things like descriptions, checkboxes and attachments.

The last step just tells you that you are ready to go.

Once you click keep building your board, you'll see the full Trello board.

Before continuing, I'll pause to point out that this book covers the web version of Trello, but Trello has a native Mac and Windows app, and native mobile app. They all work exactly the same. And they all sync together! So if you do something on your iPad, it changes on the web version. Why use a native version (vs. the web version)? It's a little more intuitive and responsive.

Trello works seamlessly wherever you are.

CHANGING YOUR BACKGROUND

I'm sure you are just dying to get into the wonderful world of boards, but before we do so, let's give Trello some personality by seeing how to change your board background.

One note before I show you this: everyone sees your background who is a member of your board. So if you are sharing a board with a team, you probably don't want to change the background to your personal family photos. For private boards, have fun! For business boards, it's usually best to stick with neutral colors.

To get started, open up the board you want the background on, click the Show menu... button in the upper right. Finally, select Change Background.

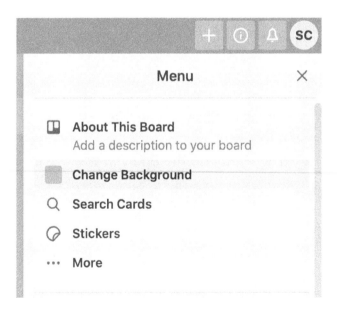

You have three choices: Photos, Colors, and Custom. Custom is only for paid subscribers and it lets you add your own photos (not the stock photos I'm about to show you).

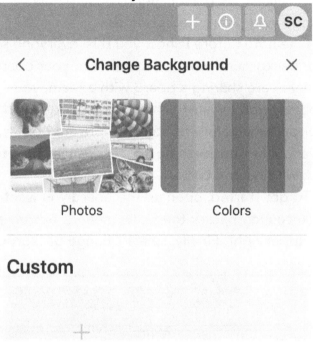

When you click Photos, you'll see dozens. You can search for what you are looking for or just browse. When you find the one you want, click it, then click the X in the upper right corner.

Your board should now have a photo background.

[2]

CRASH COURSE

This chapter will cover:
- Trello basics
- Search operators
- Board creation
- Trello templates

NAVIGATING TRELLO

Now that we know how to change our board background, let's learn basic navigation, then we'll see how to create boards, lists, and cards.

As you navigate around, you'll notice there's no Save button. Once you create it, it's saved and synced everywhere. So there's never a need to save.

Over on the upper left side are the three main navigation buttons.

The nine small squares will show you other Atlassian apps that you have connected to Trello (if any). The two most popular are Jira and Confluence. Trello is the most commercial of Atlassian's products—most of their tools have an enterprise feel and are better for larger businesses.

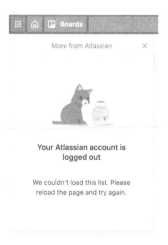

The Home button will take you to a dashboard interface with all of your boards.

The Boards button will show you a drop-down of your boards and also let you search for boards by name, which comes in handy when you start creating lots of them.

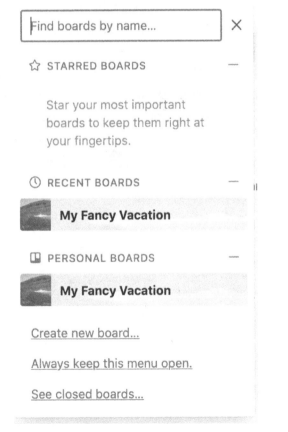

Over on the right side, the + button is where you can quickly create a board or create a team.

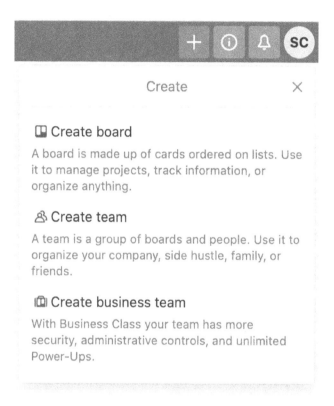

The circled "i" is the tips button; click that for little tips about using Trello.

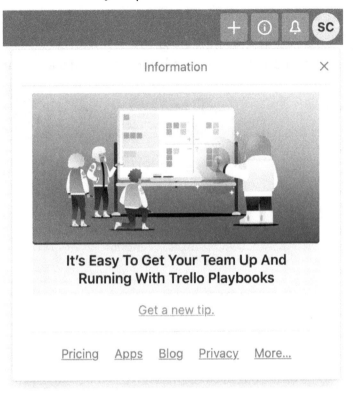

The bell button is for notifications (if any); you'll see a sleeping Taco (Trello's mascot) if you have no new notifications.

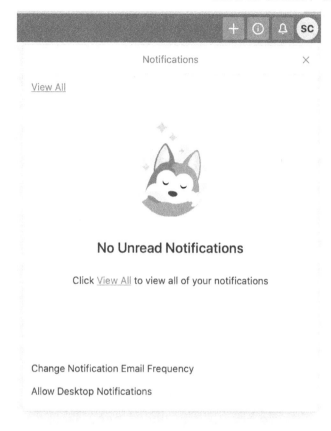

Finally, the last button is for your account settings, which we will cover later in this book.

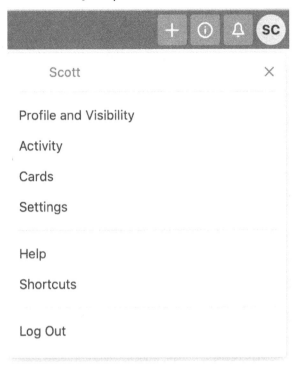

Next to boards is a search menu. Unlike the Board search, this searches everything on Trello. You can use the @ sign to search for cards and files created by specific people once you start adding them to your account.

SEARCH OPERATORS

As you search Trello you can use different search commands called "operators." Below is a list of operators currently accepted in the search (and remember, you can combine operators to re-fine the search even more).

- "-" - Adding the minus (-) in front of a search will look for cards without that operator (for example, you can say -@team_member to search for cards that don't include that team member.
- @name - looks for cards with this specific team member.
- #label - When we get into creating cards, you'll see how you can add different labels to cards. To search those labels, just add a # and type the label.
- Board:id - search for cards only on a specific board.
- List:name - search for specific lists.
- Has:attachments - looks only for cards with attachments.
- Due:day - search for cards by a specific due day. You can also add due:week to see cards due that week; due:month to see cards due that month; and due:over-due to see anything that's late.
- Create:day - lets you search for when a card was created.

- Edited:day - lets you search for cards by when they were last edited.
- Description: - lets you search for what's in a specific aspect of a card; for example, you can say checklist:eggs to search for any cards that have a checklist and the checklist item is eggs.
- Is: - Is:open - searches all open cards; is:archive searches all archived closed; is:starred searches only cards you have starred.

CREATING BOARDS

There are two places to create a board in Trello. The quickest way to add a board is to click the + button in the upper right and click Create Board.

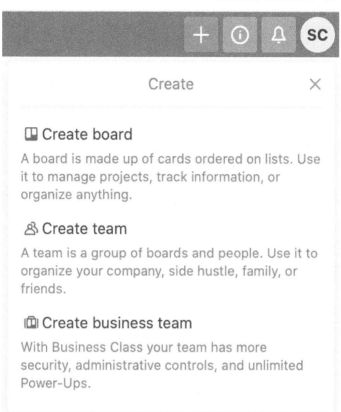

You can also create a board by clicking the Home button in the upper left, then clicking on the Create New Board next to your current board.

Once you click add a new board, there will be a very small pop-up.

To the right side, you can click the box with the three dots to change the board's background.

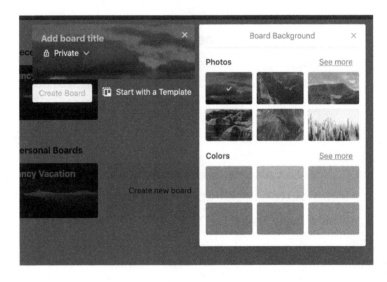

By default, the board is private; clicking on Private will open a drop-down and you can make the board public. A public board can be seen by anyone on the Internet (only you can change the content, but Trello boards do come up in Google searches if you make them Public).

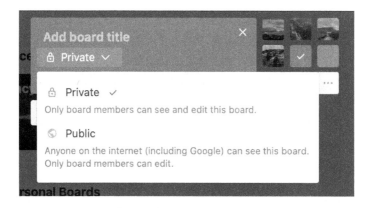

If you have teams, you can assign them to the board.

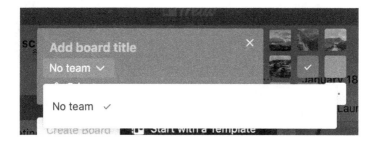

Once you give your board a name, the Create Board button will turn green and you can click it to create it.

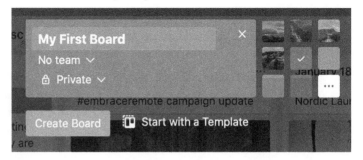

Your board is now created. It's completely blank at this point, so in the next section, we'll look at creating lists.

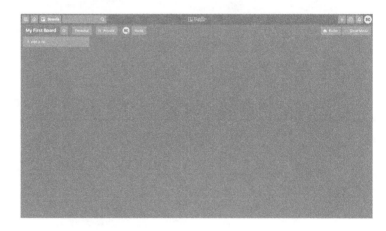

STARTING FROM A TEMPLATE

When you create a board, you'll also see an option called Start with a Template; when you click that, you'll see that Trello has dozens of boards already created for virtually any industry.

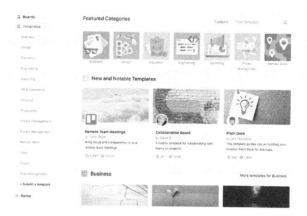

You can click on any template to read about what it is and see a little preview.

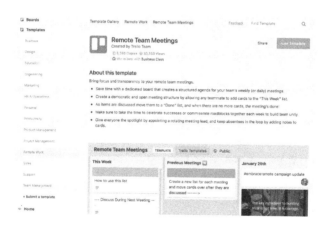

To use the template, click the green Use Template button. There are a couple of options before you add it—you can rename it, keep the cards and keep the template cards.

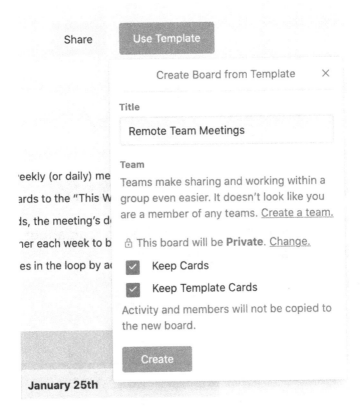

Once you click Create, you'll see the new board.

[3]

CREATING A LIST

This chapter will cover:
- Create a list
- Move a list
- Watch a list
- Archive a list

Now that you have your board, you are ready for your list. Just click the + Add a list to get started. Creating a list is very simple—add the title, click the green Add List and you are done.

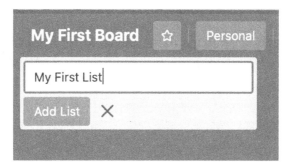

You can add an infinite number of lists by continuing to repeat the steps.

As you create more, you'll probably want to move them around. Just click and hold the list, then drag it wherever you want it to go.

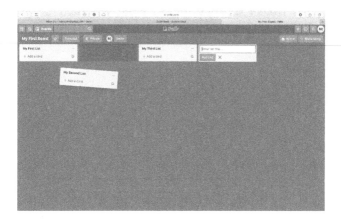

Each list has a subset of options that you can access by clicking on the three dots in the right corner of each list box.

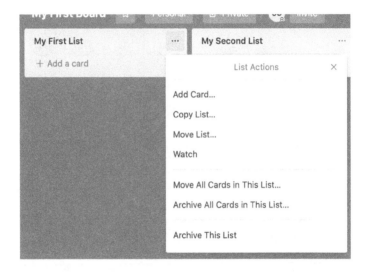

MOVE LIST

One of the more powerful options under lists options is the Move All Cards option. This lets you quickly move everything in a list to another list.

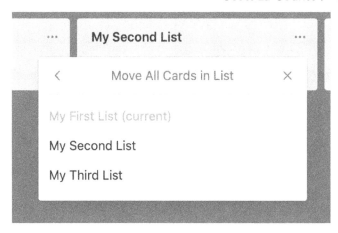

The Move List option takes it a step forward by letting you move the entire list to an entirely different board.

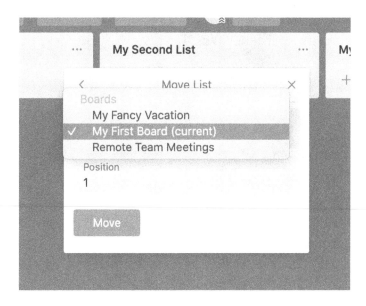

WATCH LIST

As your lists grow, you can click the Watch list icon to follow particular lists.

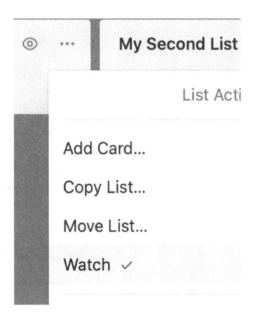

ARCHIVE LISTS

Archiving lists removes the lists and all the cards from your board, but they aren't completely deleted. It is basically hidden—removed from the board in an invisible area. You can still search for cards that were on it.

If you accidentally archive it, you can get it back by clicking on the Show Menu on the right side, then clicking the More option.

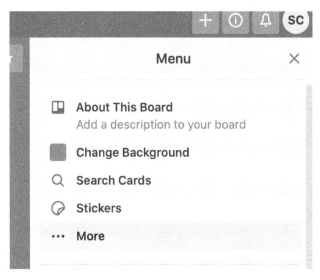

Under More, click Archived Items.

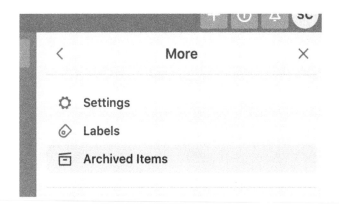

By default, this will show archived cards first; if you archived a list, click the Switch to Lists button.

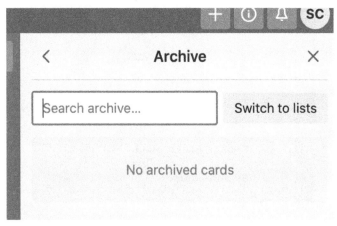

Once you see what you are looking for, click the Send to Board.

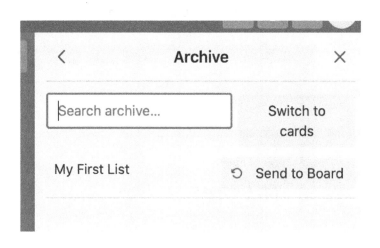

[4]

CREATING A CARD

This chapter will cover:
- Create a card
- Power-ups
- Moving / copying cards
- Sharing cards
- Card activity
- Formatting cards
- Templates

Each list can have an infinite number of cards; these cards are kind of like projects within projects; your list might be something like Vacation and your cards would be all the things to make that vacation happen. To create a card, click the + Add a card option.

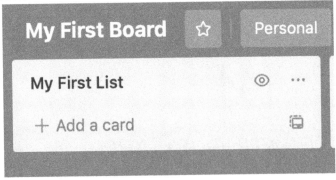

Once you title the card, you'll see the green Add card button can now be clicked.

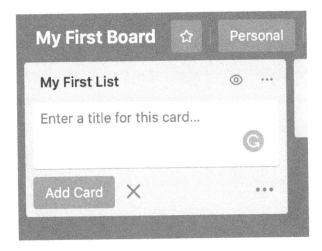

Next to the Add card button are three dots that represent more options; this lets you assign labels, member and a card position (the order it appears on the list) to the card before you add the card to your list.

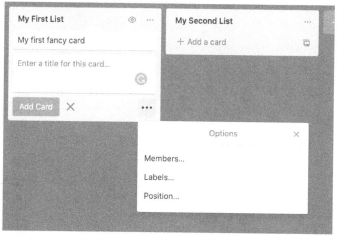

Once you add it, you can click the card one time to bring up an expanded list of options.

Clicking on any of the options will let you change something. For example, Labels lets you add labels or tags to the card.

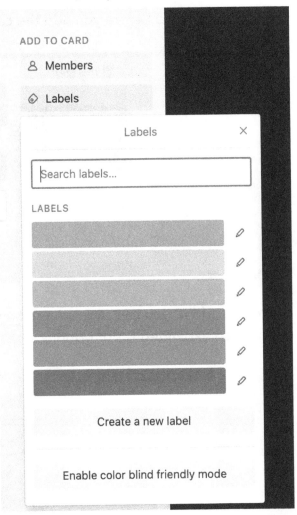

Due dates help you organize your cards so they eventually get done; you can set notifications to have reminders that a card is almost due.

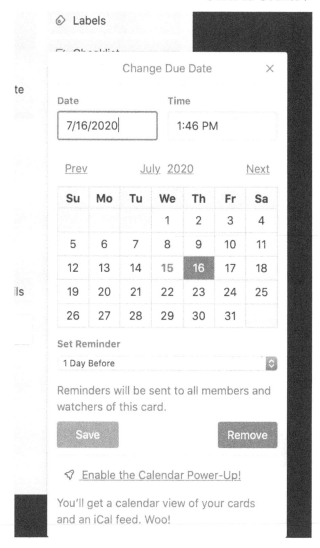

You can also attach files and links to a card. Trello integrates with most popular cloud storage solutions like Google Drive and Dropbox.

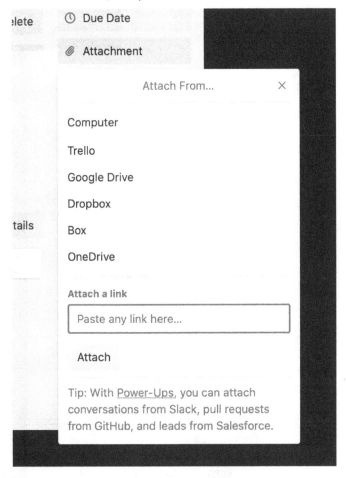

Just like you can have board backgrounds, you can also have card backgrounds. Images can get a little large on cards, and colors are much more practical. You can also attach a cover image (such as a gif if you want something animated).

CREATING A CARD CHECKLIST

A Checklist is a set of steps needed for the card to be complete. When you click this option, the first step is to name your checklist, then click Add.

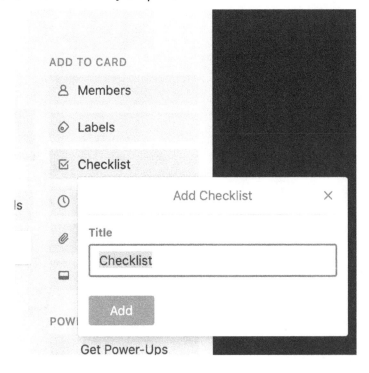

You can now start adding items to your checklist.

As you add items, you can assign them to people and also add due dates (you have to upgrade your Trello subscription to a paid plan for this option).

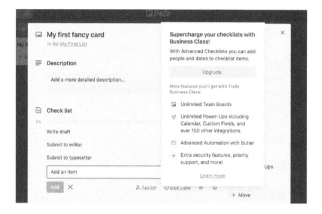

When a person checks off the item, you can monitor the progress. You can also hide completed items from showing or delete the list entirely by clicking the options above.

If you want to edit an item in a checklist, just click the title once.

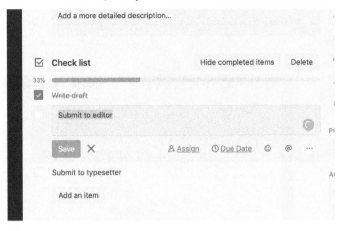

CARD POWER-UPS

Power-ups let you add integrations to your card. Power-ups are advanced (and often paid) integrations to help automate your cards or add other features.

MOVING AND COPYING CARDS

Moving and copying cards works the same way it does with lists; you can move / copy cards to other lists or you can move / copy cards to other boards.

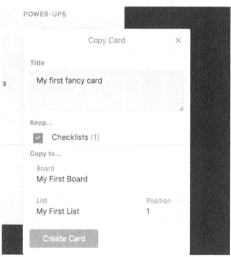

Sharing Cards

If you have another team member who is asking where your card is, there's an option at the bottom to share the card; click that, then grab the link to the card.

Archiving and Deleting Cards

Unlike lists, which you can only archive, cards you can delete. To do either, click the Archive button once. Once archives it (Send to board undoes it); once you click it once, the option to delete it will appear.

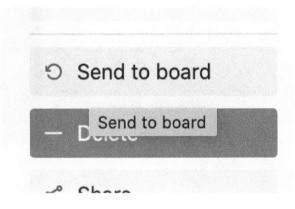

If you select Delete, it will remind you that the action cannot be undone.

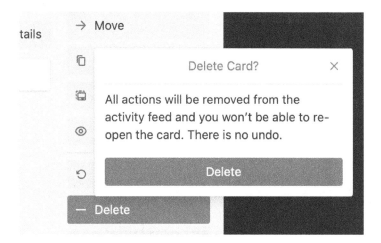

When a card is archived, you'll see a message on top of your card telling you; when it's deleted it disappears for good—no undo!

CARD ACTIVITY

At the bottom of the page, you can select Show Activity to see what actions people have performed on the card. If another team member has added something to the card or changed anything, you'll see it here.

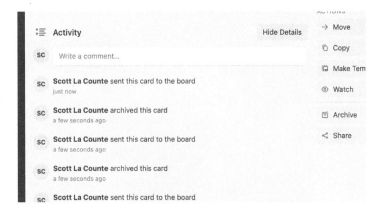

FORMATTING HELP

The description at the top can have a very basic description.

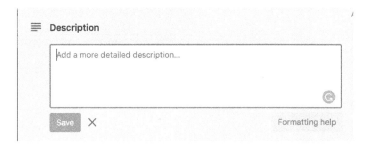

Trello has its own formatting language, however, to make the description a little nicer; if you click Formatting Help, it will show you all the possible styles that you can add to the description.

MOVING CARD

Once a card is created, you can click and drag it to any other list. The most common reason people do this is to move cards from a list for "doing" to a list for "done."

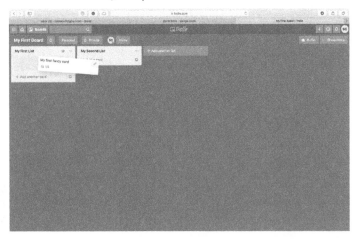

CREATE A TEMPLATE

You can also create a card from a Template. This creates a card that has preset things in place, so you don't have to repeat creating them. To get started, click the Template button to the right of + Add a card, then select Create a New Template.

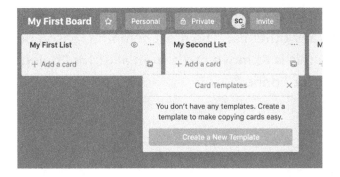

Once you add all the parameters, you are all set.

When you select that option again, you'll see the template card as an option. From here, you can click it to use it, or you can create a new template card or edit the previous template card.

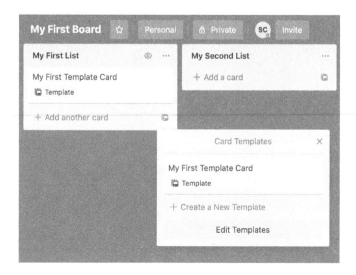

[5]
CREATING YOUR TEAM

This chapter will cover:
- Create a team
- Manage a team

Creating boards to get stuff done is nice, but Trello really shines when you work together with others. While the most obvious thing that will come to mind when you think of boards is business use, Trello can also be useful in your personal life. My wife and I have used Trello for household tasks to assign who does what and when it will get done—

we both can create and assign tasks and due dates for each other and it all syncs together.

To create a team, click the + button in the upper right corner, and click Create team (You can also create a business team, which is the same thing as a team, but with more features unlocked—you have to pay for this type of team).

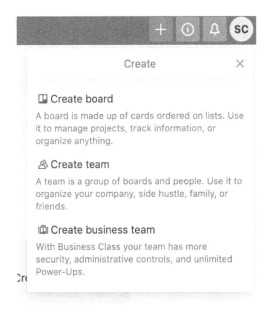

A pop-up will appear to build your first team. The first two fields are required, but you can make up any name you want. The last field (description) is not required.

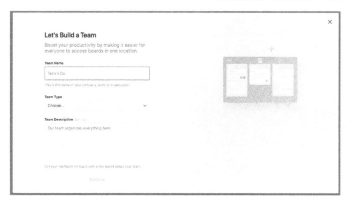

Your team type is not that important; if nothing fits, then select "Other."

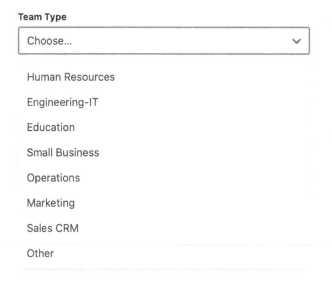

Once you have added everything, then select Continue. You'll now be able to invite people to your team, but you can also skip this part and add people later by clicking on the I'll do this later link at the bottom.

As you type in emails, you might see some show up with their names; that just means they are already a Trello user. If you don't see that, then the person needs to sign up for an account. You can add as many people as you like—you don't have to invite them one at a time—just keep adding emails until you are done. Each person (regardless if they are a Trello user) will get an email asking them to accept the invite.

Invite Your Team

Trello makes teamwork your best work. Invite your new team members to get going!

Team Members

Scott ✕

S   Scott

Invite to Team

I'll do this later

Once you invite everyone, you'll see your team dashboard. Right now it's empty because you haven't created any boards. If you have created boards, you have to assign them to your team (I'll show you how below).

At any point you can change the team's profile by clicking on Edit Team Profile. You can also give your team a logo / icon, by clicking on that icon of the two people.

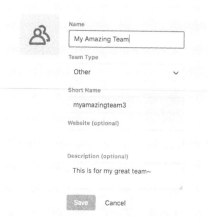

If you did not invite anyone to your team (or you want to invite more), then click on the Members tab. Here, you can also remove people from the team.

The Settings tab lets you link your team to Slack, so you can collaborate on projects within your Slack channel; you can also change if the team is private or public. If you have a paid Trello account, you'll be able to set board restrictions and assign team roles (e.g. who are admins).

Unless you are a paid member, the Business Class tab will just be an ad to upgrade; if you pay for Trello this is where you can manage things like Power-ups.

When you close this dashboard, you can access it again by clicking on the Home button in the upper left of your screen. Before, this would be a dashboard for your boards; now, however, you will see your team has been added.

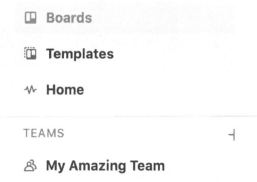

If you already have a board and want to assign it to a team, then go to the board you want to assign and click the Invite button near the middle top of the board.

You can now pick the team you want to assign it to.

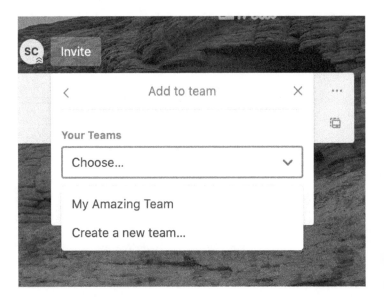

Once you click it, select Add to team.

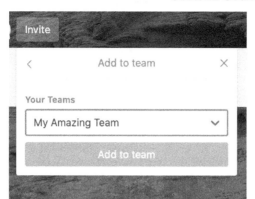

You can also invite people not on your team by creating a board link. Copy and send the link to anyone you want to see the board, and they'll have access.

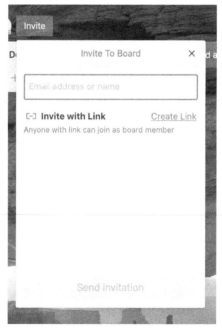

When you click on your Home button again and go to your team page, you'll see that your board is now listed under your team.

[6]
THE BUTLER

This chapter will cover:
- What is the Butler
- Butler rules
- Card buttons
- Board buttons
- Due dates

You may have noticed a little button on the right side of your board called the Butler; this is where you can go to automate your boards and create commands to make your life easier.

RULES

There are several things in the Butler; the first is Rules. A rule is a little command that you create that says, "when this happens, then make this happen." To add a rule, click the Create Rule button.

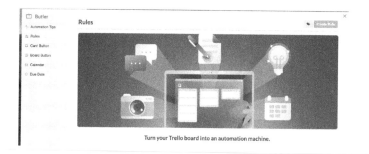

Turn your Trello board into an automation machine.

The first thing you have to do is add a trigger (i.e. "when this happens").

There are all kinds of triggers you can add. In this example, my rule will be simple: when anyone in the team moves a card.

Next, I have to find my "make this happen." In this case, my "make this happen" will be the card will get a red label. Now whenever anyone in my team moves a card, I'll see a red label on it and can quickly identify that it has been moved.

CARD BUTTONS

Card buttons let you add custom buttons to your card. Click Create Button to get started.

Before you can pick what you want your button to do, give it an icon and name.

Create a Card Button

Next, select the button's action. In this example, the button will let members quickly subscribe to the card to monitor activity.

You can edit any of these custom actions (or delete them) by clicking on the thumbnail icons next to the customization.

BOARD BUTTONS

Just like cards, you can also create buttons for your entire board.

In this example, I created a board button that lets you sort a list on the board by the date each card was created.

When you leave the Butler area, you'll see that the button is now available on your board.

When you click the button, you'll see the Butler running the command on the bottom of your screen.

CALENDAR AND DUE DATE

The last two options are for paid Trello plans only. Calendar lets you set up commands based on recurring schedules.

Due date helps you manage when your cards are due.

Butler

Automation Tips
Rules
Card Button
Board Button
Calendar
Due Date

Get help
Connected Apps
Account

Due Date Commands

Create Command

Never forget a due date.

Create commands based on a card's due date.

Stay on timeline and manage due dates on cards, stress-free

Here are some examples:

[7]

ACCOUNT SETTINGS

This chapter will cover:
- Account settings

Trello's account settings are unlike some account settings you are used to. They are simple! To get to your settings, click the round button with your initials in the upper right corner, then click Settings.

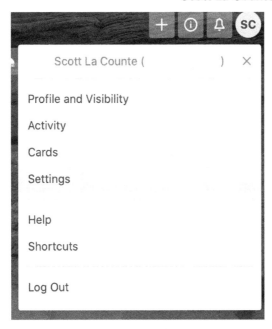

The settings are very straightforward and let you change notifications, your default language, and opt out of marking emails.

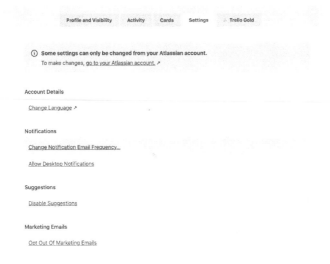

ABOUT THE AUTHOR

Scott La Counte is a librarian and writer. His first book, Quiet, *Please: Dispatches from a Public Librarian* (Da Capo 2008) was the editor's choice for the Chicago Tribune and a Discovery title for the Los Angeles Times; in 2011, he published the YA book The N00b Warriors, which became a #1 Amazon bestseller; his most recent book is *#OrganicJesus: Finding Your Way to an Unprocessed, GMO-Free Christianity* (Kregel 2016). His most recent non-technical book is *Jesus Ascended. What Does That Mean?*

He has written dozens of best-selling how-to guides on tech products.

You can connect with him at ScottDouglas.org.

9 781629 174839